DATE DUE

Printed
in USA

D1442646

Look What Came From

Germany

by

Kevin Davis

Franklin Watts

A Division of Grolier Publishing

New York London Hong Kong Sydney

Danbury, Connecticut

Series Concept: Shari Joffe
Design: Steve Marton

Library of Congress Cataloging-in-Publication Data

Davis, Kevin.
  Look What Came From Germany / by Kevin Davis.
    p. cm. — (Look what came from)
  Includes bibliographical references and index.
  Summary: Describes many things that originally come
from Germany, including inventions, vehicles, household
items, customs, animals, fairy tales, and food.
  ISBN 0-531-11685-9 (lib.bdg.)   0-531-16435-7(pbk.)
  1. German—Civilization Juvenile literature.
2.Civilization—German influences Juvenile literature.
[1. Germany—Civilization. 2. Civilization—German
influences.] I. Title.
DD17.D355   1999
943—dc21   99-19256
                                            CIP

Photo credits © : AKG London: 4 (Dieter E. Hoppe), 21; Archive Photos: cover bottom, 6 right, 10, 13; Ben Klaffke: borders on page 4, 6-32, 22 left, 24 right; Brown Brothers: 11 left; Charise Mericle: 5; Corbis-Bettmann: 12, 17 right (UPI), 1, 7 right; Envision: 16 (Mark Greenberg), cover top left, 25 bottom (Peter Johansky), 3 left, 23 right, 25 top (Rudy Muller), 15 right, 24 left (Steven Needham), 22 right, 23 left (Amy Reichman), 32 (Agence Top); Liaison Agency Inc.: 9 top right (Hulton Getty), 15 left (Roy Gumpel), 19 bottom right (Laguna Photo), 9 top left (Roger/Viollet); Nance S. Trueworthy: 27; North Wind Picture Archives: 6 left, 6 center; Peter Arnold Inc.: 19 bottom left (Franz Gorski); Photo Researchers: 3 right, 8 left (Art Attack), 19 top right (Jeanne White); PhotoEdit: cover top right, 9 bottom, 14 (Tony Freeman); Stock Montage, Inc.: 20; Superstock, Inc.: 7 left, 11 right, 17 left, 18; Tony Stone Images: cover background (Doug Armand), 19 top left (Frank Siteman); Visuals Unlimited: 8 right (Jeff J. Daly).

Visit Franklin Watts on the Internet at:
http://publishing.grolier.com

Contents

Greetings from Germany!

The flag of Germany

Germany is a beautiful country in the center of Europe. Lots of amazing things come from Germany, from hamburgers and frankfurters to automobiles and jet planes.

Germany has a long and interesting history. Thousands of years ago, many people from Northern Europe settled in Germany. About 1,500 years ago, Germany was part of the Roman Empire. Germany has gone through many wars, and was at one point divided into two countries—East Germany and West Germany. Today, Germany is one country again.

The people of Germany have brought the world many important inventions, customs, and even famous fairy tales! So let's head over to Germany to find out some of the incredible things that come from this country!

4

Inventions

A page from Gutenberg's bible

The first printing press

Johannes Gutenberg

One of the most important inventions to come from Germany was the **printing press.** This machine allowed people to print lots of pages in a short time. Johannes Gutenberg made the first printing press about 500 years ago. One of the first books he published was a Bible.

Early alarm clock

For people who had trouble waking up on time, the Germans had a great idea. They invented the **alarm clock!** The very first alarm clocks were made for monks who had to get up early in the morning to pray. The alarms were actually little bells.

Another important invention for keeping time was the **watch.** About 400 years ago, a German man created a small spring-operated watch so that people wouldn't have to carry around large clocks.

Watch from the 1600s

Thermometer

more inventions

Bayer aspirin

HANDY
°F

-TEMP
°C

120
100
80
60
40
FREEZE
20
0
20
40
60

50
40
30
20
10
0
10
20
30
40

Tayler

If you've ever been sick, you've probably had your temperature taken with a thermometer. On many thermometers, the temperature is measured in **Fahrenheit degrees.** Gabriel Fahrenheit invented this system of measuring hot and cold about 300 years ago.

Have you ever seen an **X-ray picture?** About 100 years ago, a German scientist named Wilhelm Röntgen discovered this amazing way of taking pictures of people's bones. Doctors use X-rays to see inside our bodies and detect diseases or broken bones.

Many people take **aspirin** to ease their aches and pains. About 100 years ago, German scientists first made this medicine in the form of a pill. The company that made it was named Bayer, and Bayer is now one of the most famous brands of aspirin in the world.

For thousands of years, people made tea by heating water and waiting for it to boil. In the 1920s, a German man came up with the idea for a **whistling tea kettle** that would

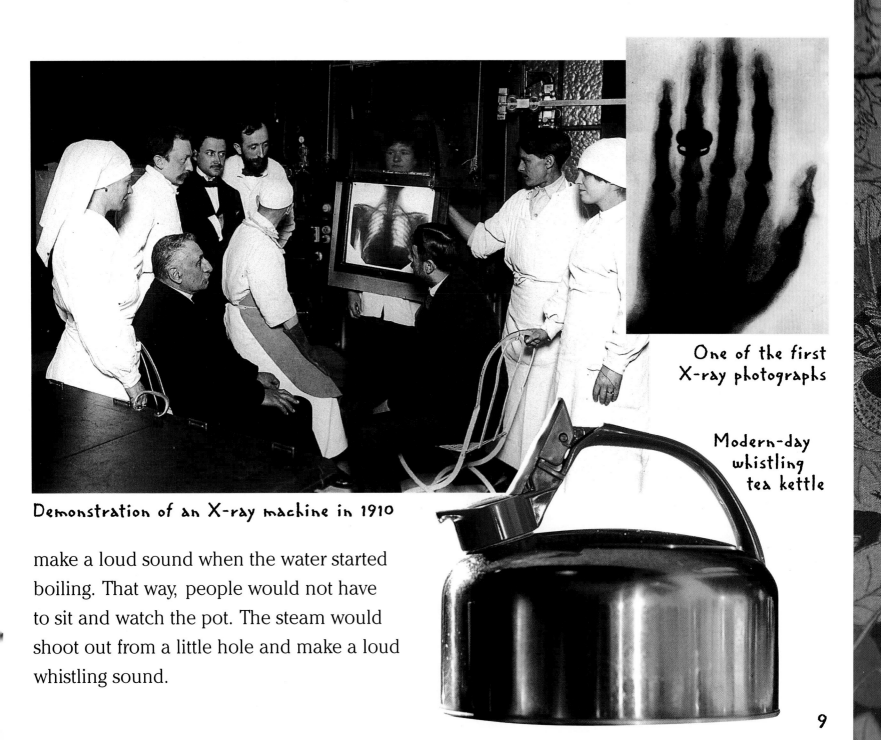

Demonstration of an X-ray machine in 1910

One of the first X-ray photographs

Modern-day whistling tea kettle

make a loud sound when the water started boiling. That way, people would not have to sit and watch the pot. The steam would shoot out from a little hole and make a loud whistling sound.

9

Transportation

One of the most important developments in the history of transportation came from Germany nearly 100 years ago. It was the **automobile!** Many inventors tried to make their own automobiles. German engineers Karl Benz and Gottlieb Daimler were the first to make a successful gasoline-powered car.

The first automobile

While testing out the gasoline engine, Daimler also built the first **motorcycle.** This two-wheeled cycle was made of wood and was very slow and clumsy. Daimler thought that mail carriers could use it to get around to deliver the mail.

The Autobahn as it looks today

The first motorcycle

Roads have been around for thousands of years, but after the invention of automobiles, people needed a smooth and fast way to get around. The first **highway** was built in Germany in 1921. This famous highway, called the Autobahn, was built in Berlin and was first designed as a race track. There is no speed limit on the Autobahn.

more transportation

The first helicopter

The Messerschmitt 262, the first jet plane to be used in combat

Many inventors came up with the idea for a **helicopter,** but the Germans were the first to make one that worked. A company called Focke-Achgelis made the first helicopter in 1937. This amazing flying machine could go up and down, backwards and forwards, and sideways!

Airplanes had already been invented when the Germans made the first **jet engine** in 1939. This very powerful engine allowed planes to move at incredible speeds! The jet engine was first used by Germans for military planes during World War II.

Around the House

Detergent

People have used soap to clean things for thousands of years. But soap often left a residue that was hard to rinse off. Germans invented **detergent** in the 1890s to solve this problem. The special mixture of chemicals was great for cleaning clothes and kitchen items.

After the invention of detergent, another important cleaner was made in Germany. You probably use it yourself. It's called **shampoo!** People found that soap did a poor job of removing the natural oils from people's hair, and these oils caused the hair to collect dirt. Shampoo was invented to get people's hair cleaner.

Boy using shampoo

Cologne

Have you ever used cologne to make yourself smell nice? The first bottled cologne was made in Germany about 300 years ago. It was named after the town of Cologne, where it was invented. A barber made the first cologne by mixing together lemon, orange, and mint oil. People loved the smell!

Customs

Children all over the world celebrate their birthdays with a birthday cake and birthday candles. Did you know that this tradition came from Germany about 800 years ago? German families celebrated birthdays with a holiday called *Kinderfest*. The party began early in the morning, when children were presented with a cake and candles. The candles were kept lit all day until dinner! The Germans also started the custom of blowing out all the candles while making a wish.

A girl blowing out the candles on her birthday cake

Christmas is celebrated in many countries, but the tradition of putting up a **Christmas tree** started in Germany. About 500 years ago, German people began decorating trees at Christmastime with such things as paper flowers, apples, cookies, and even sugar! The Germans called such a tree the *Christbaum,* which meant "Christ tree." Soon, the tradition spread around the world.

People watching a groundhog come out of his hole on Groundhog Day

Another interesting tradition that comes from Germany is **Groundhog Day.** German farmers believed that if a groundhog saw his shadow after coming out of his hole at the end of winter, then winter would last six more weeks. Farmers saw this as a sign that they should wait to plant their crops. Today, Groundhog Day is celebrated on February 2.

Christmas tree

Pets

Some of the most popular dog breeds come from Germany. Many of these dogs were bred to do work for their owners. The Dachshund was used to hunt small animals. Schnauzers were trained to kill rats and help their owners herd sheep and cattle. The German shepherd also was bred to tend sheep.

Have you ever seen a poodle? This dog was named after the German word for "puddles" because poodles were trained to retrieve ducks from the water for hunters! Other dogs, such as the big Great Dane and the Doberman pinscher, were trained to act as guards.

Miniature Schnauzer

Dachshunds

German shepherd

Great Dane

Poodles

Doberman pinscher

19

Children's Stories

Have you every heard the story **"Snow White and the Seven Dwarfs"**? Or how about **"Sleeping Beauty"**? These and many other fairy tales come from Germany. They were collected by two brothers, Jacob and Wilhelm Grimm. People in Germany had told these

"Snow White and the Seven Dwarfs"

"Cinderella"

HÄNSEL UND GRETEL

Gezeichnet von Hellmut Eichrodt. Wiedererzählt von Josefa Metz.

Verlag von A. Molling & Comp., Hannover

"Hansel and Gretel"

"The Pied Piper of Hamelin"

stories to their children for hundreds of years, but had never written them down. In the 1800s, the Brothers Grimm collected these stories and published them in books that are read by children all over the world today.

Some of the other stories from Germany include "Cinderella," "Hansel and Gretel," and "The Pied Piper of Hamelin," which is named after a real town in Germany.

Food

German men eating bratwursts

People in Germany love to eat big and hearty meals. Some of the foods that many of us enjoy today came from Germany hundreds of years ago.

Germany is famous for its sausages. Even though sausages were made by people in other countries, Germans have the biggest variety of these tasty treats—as many as 500 different kinds! Germans make sausages from beef, pork, and veal.

Frankfurter

German sausage is liverwurst. It is made from liver and is spread on bread to make sandwiches.

Do you like to eat delicious and juicy hamburgers? The hamburger was first called the "Hamburg steak" because it was first served in the German city of Hamburg. Today, the hamburger is one of the world's most popular foods.

One popular kind is called bratwurst. Probably the most famous German sausage is the frankfurter, which comes from a city in Germany called Frankfurt. In the United States, frankfurters are often called "hot dogs." Another kind of

Hamburger

more food

Sauerkraut
with German sausages

Have you ever tasted
sauerkraut? This dish of
shredded cabbage soaked in
vinegar makes your mouth pucker!
The German word *sauerkraut*
means "sour cabbage." Many people
like to put sauerkraut on top of their
frankfurters and bratwurst.

Pumpernickel bread

A popular bread from Germany is **Pumpernickel.** This dark-brown bread is similar to rye bread and is great for making ham sandwiches.

One of the tastiest desserts from Germany is **strudel.** This delicious pastry is filled with nuts, fruit, or cheese. One of the most popular kinds of strudel is apple strudel.

Another popular dessert from Germany is **Black Forest cake,** a delicious treat that has layers of chocolate sponge cake spread with black-cherry jam and whipped cream. It is named after a real forest in Germany.

Black Forest cake

See how printing works

Johannes Gutenberg's printing press was one of the world's most important inventions, but the idea behind it is actually very simple. First he made separate metal letters. These were then set next to one another to form words on a wooden printing press. Ink was applied to the surface of the letters on the press, and then paper was applied to the press.

It's easy to see for yourself how printing works. All you need to do is spread ink or paint on an object and then press it on paper to make an image. You can print different shapes and images with just about anything!

Printing with Food

Here's what you'll need:

• Fresh, uncooked fruits and vegetables with hard textures, such as apples, potatoes, carrots, peppers, or corn

• Uncooked dried pasta in different shapes: macaroni, rotini, wheel-shaped, etc.

• Newspapers

• Tempera paint

• Paper to print on

• Trays or paper plates to hold paint

• Paintbrushes

26

1. Spread out newspapers on a table to protect your work area.

2. Have an adult cut or slice potatoes, carrots, apples, and peppers crosswise. You'll find interesting hidden shapes inside the apples and peppers!

3. Dip the cut side of the fruit or vegetable into paint, or brush paint onto it.

4. Press it onto the paper and lift up. You'll see an image!

5. You can also roll a piece of corn in paint and then roll it onto the paper. Use pieces of macaroni or other pasta dipped in paint to make printed shapes, too.

How do you say...?

German and English come from the same family of languages. As you can see, some German words are similar to English words.

English	German	How to pronounce it
good morning	guten Tag	GUTTen-TAAK
goodbye	auf Wiedersehen	owf-VEE-der-zay-en
thank you	danke	DAHNK-e
alarm clock	Wecker	VECK-er
automobile	Auto	OW-to
birthday	Geburtstag	ge-BURTS-tahg
bread	Brot	broat
cake	Kuchen	COOCH-en
children	Kinder	KIN-duhr
fairy tale	Märchen	MARE-chen
motorcycle	Motorrad	motor-rahd
watch	Uhr	ooer

To find out more

Here are some other resources to help you learn more about Germany:

Books

Arnold, Helen. **Postcards From: Germany.** Raintree/Steck-Vaughn, 1997.

Boast, Clare. **Next Stop: Germany.** Heineman Library, 1998.

Byers, Helen, and Haskins, Jim. **Count Your Way Through Germany.** Carolrhoda Books, 1991.

Peters, Sonja. **Families Around the World: A Family from Germany.** Raintree/Steck-Vaughn, 1998.

Pluckrose, Henry Arthur. **Picture a Country: Germany.** Franklin Watts, 1998.

Stein, Richard Conrad. **Cities of the World: Berlin.** Children's Press, 1997.

Haviland, Virginia. **Favorite Fairy Tales Told in Germany.** Beach Tree Paperback Books, 1994.

Organizations and Online Sites

German Embassy and German Information Center
http://www.germany-info.org
This site has history, travel information, news, weather, and many great links to other sites about Germany.

CityNet Germany
http://city.net/countries/germany
CityNet is a great starting point to learn more about Germany. It has maps and links to other sites, including German cities and states.

Destination Germany
http://www.lonelyplanet.com.au/dest/eur/ger.htm
A travel guide from Lonely Planet books that has a slide show, facts at a glance, and special attractions.

Microsoft Expedia: Germany
http://www.msn.com/wg/places/germany/HFHS.htm
Another great travel guide with fast facts, pictures, maps, and links to other sites.

Glossary

ache a feeling when a part of the body hurts

breed to reproduce animals that have certain characteristics

combat battle between soldiers

custom the usual way of doing things

detect find

development growth

ease soothe, lessen

military armed forces

monk a man who has taken religious vows and lives in a separate community with other monks

publish to print words or pictures on paper

residue something that is left behind

retrieve to get and bring back

Roman Empire an ancient civilization centered in what is today Italy

strudel a pastry made from a thin sheet of dough rolled up with filling and baked

tradition a custom or way of doing things handed down from generation to generation

Index

Look what doesn't come from Germany!

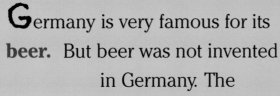

Germany is very famous for its **beer.** But beer was not invented in Germany. The ancient Egyptians are believed to have been the first to brew beer, about 4,000 years ago.

Meet the Author

Kevin Davis loves to travel and write about the interesting places he has visited. He lives in Chicago and is an author and journalist. This book is dedicated to Warren Karlenzig, another world traveler, whose ancestors came from Germany.